Britten

THE GREAT COMPOSERS

BRITTEN

by

IMOGEN HOLST

FABER AND FABER

24 Russell Square

London

First published in mcmlxvi
by Faber and Faber Limited
24 Russell Square London W.C.1
Second impression May mcmlxvi
Printed in Great Britain by
Latimer Trend & Co Ltd Plymouth

Contents

Illustrations

Illustrations

Music Examples

(The examples are all by Britten. Those marked *
are photographed from his own handwriting)

Acknowledgements

I wish to express my thanks to the following, who have kindly allowed me to reproduce copyright material: to the Oxford University Press for a verse from *Corpus Christi Carol*; to Boosey and Hawkes Music Publishers Limited for 'A New Year Carol' from *Friday Afternoons*, 'Pan' from *Six Metamorphoses after Ovid*, 'Swiss Clock' from *Alpine Suite*, 'Agnus Dei' from *Missa Brevis* and extracts from *A Hymn to the Virgin*, 'Old Abram Brown' from *Friday Afternoons*, *Rejoice in the Lamb*, *Saint Nicolas*, *The Little Sweep* and *Gloriana*; to Faber and Faber Ltd. for extracts from *Nocturnal* and *Curlew River* and for quotations from chapters by Aaron Copland, Mstislav Rostropovich and Ludwig Prince of Hesse and the Rhine in *Tribute to Benjamin Britten on his Fiftieth Birthday* (edited Anthony Gishford), from John Ireland's chapter in *British Composers in Interview* (edited Murray Schafer) and from W. H. Auden's *Collected Shorter Poems*; to Jonathan Cape Ltd. for a quotation from William Plomer's *Double Lives*; to *Tempo* (American edition, April 1940) for a quotation from 'An English Composer sees America'; to *The Listener* for extracts from articles by E. M. Forster (May 29th, 1941) and Benjamin Britten (November 7th, 1946); to *The Observer* for quotations from 'Britten by Tippett' (November 17th, 1963); to *The Sunday Telegraph* for several extracts from 'Britten Looking Back' (November 17th, 1963); to *The Leiston Observer and Mercury* (October 26th, 1962) for speeches made at the Freedom of Aldeburgh ceremony; to Gresham's School, for information from the school magazine (1929–30); to Mary Potter for the drawings on pages 59 and 61; to Meg Stevens for line illustrations on pages 28, 31, 40, 55, 65 and 73; to the Radio Times Hulton Picture Library for Plate II (b) and (c); to *Life* Magazine for Plate II (a) (photograph George Rodger, © 1947 *Time* Inc.); to the Decca Record Co. Ltd. for Plate IV; and to the Aldeburgh Festival for Plate III (b) and for two of the late Kurt Hutten's photographs (Plate III (a) and the cover).

Acknowledgements

I am very grateful to Benjamin Britten for allowing me to use his unpublished 'Beware', 'Valse in B major' and the page from *Quatre Chansons Françaises*, and for lending me manuscripts for the five facsimiles and photographs for Plate I (a), (b), (c) and (d).

I

Home

Edward Benjamin Britten was born in Lowestoft, Suffolk, on 22nd November 1913, the feast day of St. Cecilia, patron saint of all musicians. It was the right place as well as the right day for the birth of an East Anglian composer. His parents' house faced the North Sea, and the winter days and nights were filled with the buffeting of the cold north-east wind and the sound of the huge waves breaking on the pebbles and the distant squawks and screeches of the herring-gulls swooping and circling above the fishing-boats.

The sound of that sea can often be heard in his music. It would be appropriate, in a book about him, to be able to state that it was the very first sound to reach his ears. Unfortunately the statement would not be true. The first conscious sound he heard was the sound of war. A bomb had fallen on the field just opposite, and he woke to the threatening roar of an explosion. He can still remember the terror of that moment. And, bound up with the terror, he remembers the relief when his Suffolk-born nurse came to reassure him with all her native courage and kindliness.

The first music he heard was the sound of his mother singing to him. She was an amateur with a clear, true soprano voice; the friends who came to the musical evenings in her drawing-room enjoyed listening while she sang lieder by Schubert and Schumann, arias by Bach and Handel, scenes from Mozart's operas, new English songs by Frank Bridge and John Ireland, and folk songs, such as 'Oh no, John' and 'The Keys of Heaven'.

Mrs. Britten was the honorary secretary of the Lowestoft Choral Society. She helped to organize local rehearsals and performances of *The Messiah*, *The Creation* and *Elijah*, and when professional soloists came down from London she used to invite them to stay in the house. Her youngest son was able to listen to them practising, and he soon made friends with them. It was the right sort of life for a future composer to be brought up in a home where the family made music.

Home

Lowestoft

He was five when he began composing. Many years later, when *Peter Grimes* was being performed in opera houses throughout Europe, he gave a broadcast talk to schools, describing his earliest attempts to write music. 'I remember the first time I tried,' he said, 'the result looked rather like the Forth Bridge . . . hundreds of dots all over the page connected by long lines all joined together in beautiful curves. I am afraid it was the pattern on the paper which I was interested in and when I asked my mother to play it, her look of horror upset me considerably. My next efforts were much more conscious of *sound*. I had started playing the piano and wrote elaborate tone poems usually lasting about twenty seconds, inspired by terrific events in my home life such as the departure of my father for [a day in] London, the appearance in my life of a new girl friend, or even a wreck at sea. My later efforts luckily got away from these [purely] emotional inspirations.'

His mother gave him his first piano lessons. Then, when he was eight, he learnt from Miss Ethel Astle, an excellent teacher at the small school where he went with his elder sister Beth. (His brother Robert was already at a public school, and his sister Barbara was grown up.) The piano lessons were such a success that he was soon able to accompany his mother's songs and to play exciting duets with Mr. Coleman, who was organist of St. John's Church where the family went every Sunday.

His father was not a musician, but he liked listening to the singing and playing that went on in the drawing-room. He never wanted a wireless set or a gramophone in the house, because he thought it might prevent people from making music for themselves. He was a dental surgeon, and although

14

it is thirty years since he died he is still remembered in Suffolk with gratitude and affection. On train journeys between Aldeburgh and Ipswich I sometimes hear strangers talking about him and describing his gentleness and the way in which he managed to give his patients confidence. He had a quick brain and skilful hands and an immense capacity for hard work. He was a great reader, and when he could get away from his work he enjoyed reading Dickens and his other favourite authors with his children. There were occasional glorious days when he was able to borrow a boat and take the whole family out sailing. There were also long days of walking in the country when he taught his children to stride with their short legs along the Suffolk lanes and footpaths that he knew so well.

The children spent their summer holidays in a farmhouse belonging to their nurse's uncle. It was near Butley, about thirty miles south of Lowestoft. Here the walks were across the marshes, with the wind blowing from the sea. As they went on their way, the tall reeds and rushes moved with them, leaning over with a swishing sound, while high overhead the curlews and redshanks called to each other. Beyond the marshes, the farthest walks led to Shingle Street, a small row of cottages on a pebbly beach, where there was nothing in sight except a vast expanse of sea and sky. Shingle Street has altered very little since those Augusts at the end of the First World War. The stony shelf of pebbles stretches for mile after mile into the distance. On a still day, the light can have the delicate outlines of a Japanese picture. On a stormy day, even in summer, the grey sea batters itself against the shelf, dragging the shingle down with a scrunching, grating, slithering sound. To anyone who lives on the Suffolk coast, this sound means home.

II

Prep School

South Lodge Preparatory School was only five minutes' walk from Benjamin Britten's home in Lowestoft, so he was allowed to attend as a day-boy although the school was really meant for boarders. This privilege had its disadvantages. It cut him off from the sociable life of a boarding school while depriving him of nearly all the blessings of living at home. School hours were from early morning until bed-time. He went home just to sleep, and for weeks on end he saw hardly anything of his parents. By the time he was in the upper school he was having to stay until nine o'clock every evening to do extra preparation with the other boys who had the best brains in the school. For he was good at his lessons, particularly at mathematics, and the headmaster hoped that he would win a scholarship.

In spite of this extremely full life he somehow managed to fit in a great deal of composing without letting it interfere with his school work, or with his games which he was passionately keen on. He must have written most of his music before breakfast, for there are stacks and stacks of manuscripts dating from these years. He used to write out specially neat copies of all the songs and instrumental pieces that he considered worthy of including in the bound volumes he gave to his parents. Among the earliest songs are settings of 'Beware!', 'If I'd as much money as I could spend', 'Wandering Willie', and 'Oh that I'd ne'er been married'. He set poems by Tennyson, Shelley, Shakespeare and Kipling, pieces from the Bible, bits of plays, and occasionally poems in French.

His piano pieces, even if they were only eight bars long, were always real piano music. By this time he was also learning the viola, and the music he wrote for strings shows that he had the feel as well as the sound of the instruments in his mind. Every detail of bowing was carefully marked. Whatever he was writing for, his players or singers were given full directions for performance. Pianists were told when to take off the pedal; organists were told what registration to use. Each slur and staccato dot and crescendo

From a volume of songs written in 1922–3

and diminuendo was clearly indicated as an essential part of the music.

On his ninth birthday one of his uncles had given him Stainer's 'Rudiments' bound in dark red cloth with a picture of St. Cecilia embossed in gold on the cover. He must have studied it from beginning to end, memorizing a vast amount of information. From then onwards, Italian terms appear in all his compositions, from 'rubato moltissimo' to the rarely-used 'mancando'. (Thirty years later he found few orchestral players were able to understand the less obvious of his Italian terms, and he decided he would have to write them in English in future.)

Metronome marks are also shown in these early pieces, and at a change of time-signature from two-two to three-four it is clearly indicated that the speed of the new dotted minim should equal that of the previous minim. His family motto was 'Never unprepared', and he certainly lived up to it. He learnt an immense amount just from reading all the printed music he could get hold of. One of his greatest treats, whenever the whole family had a day in London, was to be given three-and-sixpence and to be allowed to look through dozens of miniature scores at Augener's music shop before choosing the one that he wanted to buy.

Reading music was a solitary occupation, and occasionally there were technical details that could lead him astray: at one time he believed that every piece of music had to last until it had reached the end of the bottom line of the page, and he must have been enormously relieved when he discovered that a composer could stop where he liked and that it was the publisher's job to space the music so that it used up the whole page.

He had begun having harmony lessons when he was ten. (Other beginners will be glad to know that he sometimes wrote forbidden consecutives and had to correct his exercises for the next week's lesson.) The strictness of the textbook rules could do no damage to the freedom of his own compositions: he continued to pour out a stream of cheerful, flowing, gracious tunes such as the 'Valse' on page 19, which is one of the early pieces he borrowed when he was grown-up for his *Simple Symphony* for string orchestra.

Being brought up in a home without a gramophone or a wireless set, he had few opportunities for getting to know any twentieth-century works: he heard nothing at South Lodge School, for the music there was practically non-existent. The first piece of 'modern' music he came across was my father's 'Song of the Ship-builders'. He found it in a music shop in Lowestoft when he was looking for duets that his mother could sing with her friends, and he was thrilled by its dark augmented seconds and its subtle enharmonic changes and its rhythmical *ostinato* bass. Then, in 1924, he was taken to the Norwich Triennial Festival to hear Frank Bridge conduct his orchestral suite *The Sea*. This was a revelation. As a result of hearing such exciting music his own pieces became longer and longer, and more and more ambitious.

The ninety-one pages of the full score of his *Overture in B flat minor* for full orchestra were written in nine days, during end-of-term examinations

From a volume of *Valses* written in 1923

and school sports and cricket matches. He was twelve by then, and his parents realized that they would have to find a more experienced teacher for him. By great good fortune the right teacher, Frank Bridge, came back to East Anglia at just the right moment. Years later, Britten described their first meeting and the unforgettable lessons in composition. 'It turned out', he wrote, 'that my viola teacher, Audrey Alston, was an old friend of Bridge's . . . and when the success of *The Sea* brought him to Norwich again in 1927 with a specially written work called *Enter Spring*, I was taken to meet him. We got on splendidly, and I spent the next morning with him going over some of my music. From that moment I used to go regularly to him, staying with him in Eastbourne or in London, in the holidays from my prep school . . . I badly needed his kind of strictness; it was just the right treatment for me. His loathing of all sloppiness and amateurishness set me standards to aim for that I've never forgotten. . . . The lessons were mammoth. I remember one that started at half past ten, and at tea-time Mrs. Bridge came in and said, "Really, you *must* give the boy a break" . . . I was perhaps too young to take in so much at the time, but I found later that a good deal of it had stuck firmly. . . . Bridge insisted on the absolutely clear relationship of what was in my mind to what was on the paper. I used to get sent to the other side of the room; Bridge would play what I'd written and demand if it was what I'd really meant. . . . I continued to write a vast amount under his guidance—orchestral music, string quartets, piano music and many songs, of which the only one to survive publicly is "The Birds". I had a terrible struggle with this before finding what has been called "the right ending in the wrong key". Bridge made me go on and on at it, worrying out what hadn't come right, until I spotted that the cycle of changing keys for each verse needed such an ending. . . . By the time I was thirteen or fourteen I was beginning to get more adventurous. Before then what I'd been writing had been sort of early nineteenth century in style; and then I heard Holst's *Planets* and Ravel's string quartet and was excited by them. I started writing in a much freer harmonic idiom.'

One of the most adventurous of these freer works was his *Quatre Chansons Françaises* for soprano solo and orchestra, written in the summer of 1928 during his last term at South Lodge, and dedicated to his parents on the twenty-seventh anniversary of their wedding. The poems were by Victor Hugo and Paul Verlaine. He had been reading a good deal of French poetry, and it happened that one of the poems he had been exploring was set as a French unseen translation in his public school entrance examination. This proved very useful, for he had been writing so much music that he had found it difficult to keep up with all his revision.

The days were more strenuous than ever before. He was head prefect, and he took his responsibilities very seriously. He had been intensely worried by the bullying that went on in the school, and he found that some of the thirteen-year-old boys had been beating the smaller ones. He was not by nature a fighter of causes but he was determined to do all that he could about it, and during his last term he managed to get some of the bullying stopped.

Games as well as work took up a great deal of time. He was already *Victor Ludorum,* and it looked as though he was also going to be *Primus inter pares.* But at the very last minute he got into disgrace. The subject of the end-of-term essay was 'Animals', and he seized hold of the opportunity to write a passionate protest, not only against hunting, but also against any form of organized cruelty, including war. The school authorities were shocked. His essay was marked with a 'Nought'. Such a thing had never been known to happen, and he left South Lodge under a cloud of disapproval.

A page from the full score of *Quatre Chansons Françaises*, July 1928

III

Public School

Unfortunately he began his first day at his public school under another cloud. Gresham's School at Holt, in Norfolk, was only forty miles from Lowestoft, so his parents took him there by car at the beginning of term and left him to wait for all the other boys who were coming by train. While he was wandering round the playing-fields and wondering what the new life was going to be like, a sudden shadow crossed his path and a tall, frowning man came up to him, saying, 'So *you* are the little boy who likes Stravinsky!' This, he learnt, was the music master.

In spite of such an unpromising introduction to his new school, he found that Gresham's had its good points. Although it was not in Suffolk it was still in East Anglia, and there were real fields and real woods to walk in. The school was run on liberal-socialist lines, and the boys had a certain amount of freedom and were encouraged to think for themselves. Caning was condemned, at any rate in theory. (The 1929 editor of the school magazine was able to say: 'The principle of "spare the rod and spoil the child", though dying hard, is nevertheless dying. It will be a great day when, for the last time, a vigilant schoolmaster imagines that he can gain his pupil's gratitude and affection, or increase his mental efficiency, by hurting him six times, or if that fails, by hurting him twelve times.') The Officers' Training Corps was voluntary, and a conscientious objector could state his own case. There was a distinguished group of 'non-recruits' who were among the best athletes in the school: they were allowed extra time for cricket and tennis instead of having to learn to stick bayonets into sacks of straw.

The headmaster knew very little about art but he knew that it mattered, and when the school Debating Society put forward the opinion that 'the world owes more to art than to science', the motion was only just lost by the narrow margin of six votes.

There was a school choir and orchestra, and each term several chamber-music recitals were given by the staff and the senior pupils. A paragraph in the school magazine of December 1929 says: 'At the last recital pianoforte trios by Mozart and Brahms proved a welcome change from the usual routine, and also provided us with an opportunity of hearing E. B. Britten as a viola player. He proved a very reliable musician in ensemble work.' A few months later the same writer was reporting that 'E. B. Britten's pianoforte playing was of a very high standard', and after a performance of one of his own trios, the general opinion was that 'he should go far'.

Some of his contemporaries can still remember their astonishment that anyone in the fifth form could play with such brilliance and understanding. He was having piano lessons in London from Harold Samuel, and was still going to Eastbourne during the holidays for composition lessons from Frank Bridge.

In a tribute written more than thirty years later he has put into words what Frank Bridge's influence meant to him. Writing of his visits to the Bridges' home, he says: 'It was, of course, the first time I had seen how an artist lived. I heard conversations which centred round the arts; I heard the latest poems discussed, and the latest trends in painting and sculpture. He also drove me around the south of England and opened my eyes to the beauty of the Downs with their tucked-away little villages, and to the magnificence of English ecclesiastical architecture. . . . It can be imagined what I owe to [his] guidance at this particularly impressionable time of life. . . . I had already been a pacifist at school, and a lot of my feeling about the First World War came from Bridge. He had written a piano sonata in memory of a friend killed in France; and although he didn't encourage me to take a stand for the sake of a stand, he did make me argue and argue and argue. . . . In everything he did for me, there were perhaps above all two cardinal principles. One was that you should try to find yourself and be true to what you found. The other—obviously connected with it—was his scrupulous attention to good technique, the business of saying clearly what was in one's mind. He gave me a sense of technical ambition.'

The influence of these 'cardinal principles' can clearly be heard in the two or three published works by Britten that he wrote during his last year at Gresham's. The beautiful eight-part *Hymn to the Virgin* was written while he was in the school sanatorium. (There was no music paper within reach, so he drew the staves on a page from an ordinary exercise book.) One can only hope that some of the other songs, still in manuscript, will one day be published. They include settings of poems by Blake and James Joyce which he somehow managed to find time to write during the last few days of his last summer term.

From the original manuscript of *A Hymn to the Virgin*, July 1930

He was sixteen and a half when he left school with an open scholarship for composition at the Royal College of Music in London. During that August, while he was waiting for the new term to begin, he happened to be at a tennis party in Lowestoft where one of the guests asked him what career he intended to choose. Britten said that he intended to be a composer. The tennis player was astonished. 'Oh!' he said, 'but what *else*?' It was impossible to try to explain that composing was not just a hobby. The casual, devastating remark came as a warning of what to expect in the future.

IV

The Royal College of Music

It was Frank Bridge's suggestion that while he was at college he should go to John Ireland for composition lessons. Ireland found him 'very industrious'. But some of the other professors had their doubts about him. At his scholarship examination one of the adjudicators had been heard to mutter: 'What is an English public schoolboy doing writing music of this kind?'

He himself began to have doubts about the college during the very first week of term. He had been looking forward to it all the time he was at Gresham's and had been longing for the moment when he could begin his serious training as a professional musician. But he now found himself sitting in a dictation class and finishing the test before any of the other students were half-way through the first bar. (In those days the standard of entrance to the college was very much lower than it is now.) He was brimful of energy and ideas, but when he went to a composition lesson Ireland told him to write a song 'with a note to each syllable'. The advice was offered with well-meant sincerity: in Ireland's own youth it would have been helpful, for at that time English composers were writing songs which sounded like translations from the German, and they needed to keep for a while to the time-patterns and the inflection of their own spoken language. Music, however, changes with each generation. And unfortunately there are not enough teachers who can find the time to give their own well-stored theories a spring-clean every year, throwing away the notions that are no longer any use.

One of the great disadvantages of life at the college was the lack of opportunity for the students to get to know each other. They went their separate ways, travelling for an hour or more to a twenty-minute lesson on a Tuesday morning and going straight back to their solitary lodgings, to return for a forty-minute class on the Thursday afternoon. Britten spent his time practising the piano and writing his compositions in an attic room in the boarding-house where he was living with his sister Beth. He kept away from the college, except for the few lessons that were down on his time-table. No one suggested that he might learn something useful by going to rehearsals of the opera and ballet classes in the small but excellently equipped theatre in the basement of the college. There he could have seen for himself how the members of an operatic chorus need to be placed so that their movements can be a help rather than a hindrance to the music. And in the ballet rehearsals he would have seen how difficult it could be for a dancer standing in the wings to have to leap on to an empty stage if the tune happened to begin on the down-beat of the bar. (This is one of the technical lessons Britten learnt by trial and error, more than twenty-five years later, when he conducted his ballet *The Prince of the Pagodas* at the Royal Opera House, Covent Garden.)

At college he would have liked to have learnt much more about contemporary music but there seemed so few opportunities. He looked for a score of Schoenberg's *Pierrot Lunaire* in the college library, and when he saw that it was not in the catalogue he wrote a request for it in the 'suggestions' book, but the request was turned down. This was the time when he was breaking away from the influence of nineteenth-century German music. Between the ages of thirteen and sixteen he had adored Beethoven and Brahms and had known nearly every note of their music. But by now he had discovered Purcell, whose music was very much closer to his own way of thinking and to his own natural inclinations.

Throughout his time at the college he continued to see a good deal of Frank Bridge. They used to go to concerts together at Queen's Hall, where they heard exciting first performances of new works. Bridge did his utmost to persuade the college authorities to have several of Britten's own compositions tried through at the informal concerts given by the students. But the only work of his that was performed there was his Op. 1, the *Sinfonietta* for ten instruments. When one looks through the programmes of students' works for full orchestra that were rehearsed under the Patrons' Fund scheme for young composers it seems incredible that no work of his should have been heard.

He would have learnt so much if his *Psalm 130* for chorus, brass, strings and drums could have been rehearsed by the college choir and orchestra. The experience would certainly have taught him to avoid the unnecessarily difficult passages in *A Boy was Born*, a set of variations for unaccompanied chorus, written in the winter of 1932–3 and published two years later. The work was an astonishing achievement, full of invention and imaginative

Corpus Christi Carol from *A Boy was Born*, Op. 3
(piano arrangement made in 1961)

sound. There were memorable tunes in it, su ch as the carol on page 27 But there were too many uncomfortable moments for the voices. Twenty years later he revised the work for republication, cutting out the awkward intervals and the over-insistent repetitions and the unwanted rubatos. There is not much doubt that he could have made these alterations in 1933 if he had had a chance of hearing his fellow-students struggling with the notes he had written while he was at the Royal College of Music.

In his last year at college he was awarded a small scholarship for studying abroad. He hoped to be able to go to Vienna to have lessons with Berg, whose music had made a deep impression on him. But for some reason the authorities were against it. This was a great blow at the time. Later, however, he was able to realize that it was a good thing to have had to learn the hard way, by finding things out for himself.

V

Earning a Living in London

In Britten's own description of how he first began work as a professional musician he says: 'When I was nineteen I had to set about earning my living. I was determined to do it through composition: it was the only thing I cared about and I was sure it was possible. My first opportunity was the chance of working in a film company. This was much to my taste although it meant a great deal of hard work. I had to work quickly, to force myself to work when I didn't want to, and to get used to working in all kinds of circumstances. The film company I was working for was not a big commercial one; it was a documentary company and had little money. I had to write scores for not more than six or seven players, and to make those instruments make all the effects that each film demanded. I also had to be ingenious and try to imitate the natural sounds of everyday life. I well remember the mess we made in the studio one day when trying to fit an appropriate sound to shots of a large ship unloading in a dock. We had pails of water which we slopped everywhere, drain-pipes with coal slipping down them, model railways, whistles, and every kind of paraphernalia we could think of.'

In the film called *Night Mail* he was faced with having to find the right sound for a train going through a tunnel and approaching nearer and nearer: he had the brilliant idea of recording a cymbal clash and then reversing the sound-track so that the dying-away vibrations became louder and louder, stopping just short of the actual clash. (This was one of the devices that helped to bring about the *musique concrète* of the nineteen-fifties.)

The script of *Night Mail* was by the poet W. H. Auden, who was then teaching in a boys' preparatory school. Auden had been at Gresham's several years before Britten went there: in a poem written at about the same time as *Night Mail* he looks back on his school days, when he and his friends 'spoke of books and praised/The acid and austere.'

29

Britten thought of Auden as 'a powerful, revolutionary person'. It was not only in films that they collaborated: there were also plays needing incidental music. These were produced by the Group Theatre, for which Auden, Isherwood, Eliot, Spender, MacNeice and other poets were writing during the nineteen-thirties.

Britten was by now a thoroughly professional composer, which meant that he was prepared to write whatever music he was asked for. In 1934 one of the requests was for a book of songs for the boys' school where his brother Robert was headmaster: the result was *Friday Afternoons*, a volume that is still greeted with enthusiasm in every school where it finds its way.

ROUND for four voices, from *Friday Afternoons*, Op. 7

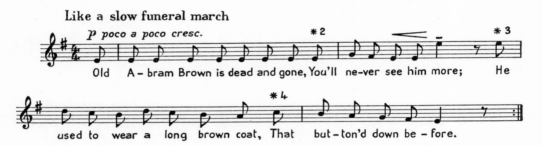

In 1936 a request came from the Norwich Festival: the organizers commissioned him to write a work for solo voice and orchestra. The result was *Our Hunting Fathers*, with a text devised by Auden on the subject of man's relations with animals. The audience at the first performance could manage to listen to the sections on animals as pests and animals as pets, but when it came to the dance of death, 'the song of the killing of animals for pleasure', most of them found the music far too uncomfortable. There were a few listeners, however, who recognized that here was a composer who could express his passionate convictions in passionate and convincing sounds.

He dedicated *Our Hunting Fathers* to his publisher, Ralph Hawkes, who had given him the best practical help that a young composer could possibly have, by offering him a contract for anything that he wrote.

Another encouraging sign was to find the International Society for Contemporary Music wanting to perform several of his works: in 1936 his *Suite for Violin and Piano* (Op. 6) was played at their Barcelona Festival, and in 1937 their Salzburg Festival gave the first performance of his *Variations on a Theme of Frank Bridge*. This was the work that made his music known to a much wider public. Within two years of the Salzburg performance it was played more than fifty times in Europe and America.

During these years his music was more favourably received abroad than in his own country. In England he was aware of the unfortunate distinction between 'music' and 'contemporary music': he had noticed that audiences, having done their duty by listening to an occasional concert of new works, would return with a sigh of relief to the normal programmes of 'music'. Auden, who was 'very much anti-bourgeois', was saying 'an artist ought either to live where he has live roots or where he has no roots at all: in England today the artist feels essentially lonely'.

Britten was not rootless, but he was homeless in the late nineteen-thirties, for the house in Lowestoft had been sold after the death of his parents. He decided to take a disused mill in the village of Snape, six miles from Aldeburgh, and have it restored. Here he could escape from London and invite his friends to stay with him. One of these friends, the American composer Aaron Copland, has described a visit in 1938: 'I can still recall the week-end I spent there and the excitement of exchanging ideas with a new-found composer friend, Benjamin Britten, then aged twenty-four. . . . I had with me the proofs of my school opera, *The Second Hurricane*, composed for young people of fourteen to seventeen. It had been performed the previous year by a group of talented students at a lower East Side settlement school in New York. It didn't take much persuasion to get me to play it from start to finish, singing all the parts of the principals and chorus in the usual composer fashion. Britten seemed pleased. Less than a year after this visit, he was on his way to North America. Perhaps our meeting in Snape had some part in his decision to try his luck abroad.'

A NEW YEAR CAROL from *Friday Afternoons*, Op. 7

1. Here we bring new wa - ter from the well __ so clear,
2. Sing reign of Fair Maid, with gold up-on her toe,
3. Sing reign of Fair Maid, with gold up-on her chin,

For to wor-ship God with this hap - py New Year.
O-pen you the West Door and turn the Old Year go.
O-pen you the East Door and let the New Year in.

Sing

Third Verse to ✠

Chorus for Verses I & II

le-vy dew, sing le-vy dew, the wa-ter and the wine; The se-ven bright gold

wires and the bu-gles that do shine.

D.S. 𝄋

Chorus for Verse III

le-vy dew, sing le-vy dew, the wa-ter and the wine; The

una corda

se-ven bright gold wires and the bu-gles that do shine.

Ped. ———— * Ped. —*

C

VI

A Visit to America

Like many English travellers to America Britten found his first glimpse of
the country 'enormously stimulating'. He was sure that young composers had more opportunities there than anywhere else in the world.
But after spending several months in New York and the Middle West
he realized that American composers, in their determination to be truly
contemporary, were inclined to be excessively national. He warned them
about it in an article he wrote for the *New York Times* in the spring of 1940,
saying: 'A complete rejection of the great European tradition is fatal, for,
after all, that tradition is nothing but centuries of experience of what
people like to hear and what players like to play. Why not make the best
of both worlds? With lessons learned from Europe, let an American style
develop naturally and without forcing, which it surely will do, if the composer takes notice of what is going on around him and writes the best music
he can for every occasion that offers itself. . . . There are school operas to
be written, and pieces for the numberless school children learning to play
instruments. . . .'

It is characteristic that he should already have been thinking about
school orchestras, but it is even more revealing to find him advising other
young composers to 'make the best of both worlds'. For this is what he
himself has been doing ever since. He has never felt the need for 'originality
at any price', knowing that the greatest composers have frequently borrowed from each other as a matter of course. In one of his recent programme
notes about Mozart he has said: 'All his life, Mozart had the wit to be
influenced by great composers, but then he assimilated these influences and
made them part of his own character.' The great composers who have
chiefly influenced Britten are Purcell, Bach, Mozart, Schubert, Verdi,
Tchaikovsky, Mahler and Berg, and their music has become part of his
character. He never bothers about keeping to an 'idiom', but uses any
device and any formula that happens to be suitable for the work he is

writing. And when other people are worrying about problems of style, and insisting that key signatures and common chords are out of date, he says: 'It doesn't matter what style a composer chooses to write in, as long as he has something definite to say and says it clearly.'

In America, in 1940, he had something startlingly definite to say in his orchestral *Sinfonia da Requiem*, written in memory of his parents, and in the *Seven Sonnets of Michelangelo*, for tenor and piano. The *Sonnets* were written for his friend Peter Pears, who had been a member of the B.B.C. Singers from 1936 to 1938 and had already toured America twice with the New English Singers. His sensitive, passionate and highly intelligent singing was exactly what Britten needed. It is rare for a song-writer to find the right singer to rehearse with him day after day. (Schubert knew how fortunate he was to be working with the great artist Vogl: in one of his letters he says 'when Vogl sings and I play, it is as if we were one and the same person'.) Pears and Britten have gone on working together ever since the *Michelangelo Sonnets*, and have reached a perfect partnership between singer and pianist.

They gave a fair number of recitals together while they were in America. But life was not easy, for they were weighed down with distress and anxiety about the war. Auden, who was also in America, had written on the day that war broke out:

> *Waves of anger and fear*
> *Circulate over the bright*
> *And darkened lands of the earth,*
> *Obsessing our private lives . . .*
> *. . . I and the public know*
> *What all schoolchildren learn,*
> *Those to whom evil is done*
> *Do evil in return.*

Auden had by now become an American citizen: his own war-service during those years was, in his own words, to 'Ruffle the perfect manners of the frozen heart, And once again compel it to be awkward and alive.' There was a time when Britten also had thought of settling in America. But he had learnt that it was impossible to go on living as an exile in a country where he had no roots. It was not only the rootlessness of being the wrong side of the Atlantic that was so depressing: it was also the un-bearable feeling of not belonging anywhere in a world at war. The strain and stress made him physically ill and for several months he was unfit for

any work. For the first and only time in his life he stopped writing music.
This is the worst thing that can happen to a composer.

There was little that his friends could say to help him: they could only
remind him that he was not alone and that other artists had been made ill
through anxiety and indecision. The poet and novelist William Plomer,
who was soon to become his friend, was already saying that 'disease is a
kind of protest of the individual against his environment, and when this
protest is against not only the way that his life, but the way that the world
is ordered, then the disease is deep-seated indeed'.

One day, while he was in California, he happened to glance at a copy
of *The Listener*, and there he saw an article by E. M. Forster on the poet
Crabbe. It said: 'To talk about Crabbe is to talk about England. He never
left our shores. . . . He did not go to London much, but lived in villages
and small country towns. [He] was born at Aldeburgh, on the coast of
Suffolk. It is a bleak little place, not beautiful. It huddles round a flint-
towered church and sprawls down to the North Sea—and what a wallop
the sea makes as it pounds at the shingle! Near by is a quay, at the side of
an estuary, and here the scenery becomes melancholy and flat; expanses
of mud, saltish commons, the marsh-birds crying. Crabbe heard that sound
and saw that melancholy, and they got into his verse.'

Even before he had finished reading that article Britten had decided that
he must get back to England as soon as he could. The decision immediately
made him feel better. And he began composing again.

The year 1942 was a difficult one for crossing the Atlantic, and he and
Peter Pears had to wait many months before they could get their passage
home. During that time they bought a copy of Crabbe's poems and read
The Borough. They were particularly impressed with the story of 'Peter
Grimes', and they began to think about turning it into an opera.

At last they were able to leave America. They made the journey in a
small Swedish cargo boat at the very end of a long convoy, and for four
weeks they had to dodge to and fro to avoid the enemy submarines and the
long-range aircraft based in occupied France. But Britten went on composing all the time. He was working at his setting of the *Hymn to St. Cecilia*
that Auden had written for him. It is a long, intricate poem, full of changing
moods, and it has a refrain that is an invocation:

> *Blessèd Cecilia, appear in visions*
> *To all musicians, appear and inspire:*
> *Translated Daughter, come down and startle*
> *Composing mortals with immortal fire.*

PLATE I

(a) *Benjamin Britten in 1925*

(b) *With a South Lodge school friend (now Major-General F.C. Barton, C.B.E.) in 1928*

(c) *With Frank Bridge in 1930*

(d) *With W. H. Auden and William Coldstream as 'The Three Graces' in 1936*

PLATE II

(a) *With Peter Pears in 1946*

(b) *In a fishing boat off Aldeburgh, with E. M. Forster, 'the Nipper', and Bill Burrell, in 1948*

(c) *The last scene in* Let's Make an Opera, *1949*

VII

The Return to Suffolk

They came back to an England that had been bombed. Old friends had died, including Frank Bridge; and several of Britten's school-friends had been killed in the war. Many young musicians were joining the Royal Air Force band, in order to combine their compulsory National Service with keeping up their technique as professional players. But Britten and Pears chose to face a tribunal as pacifists, and they were granted exemption because it was clear that they were working for their fellow-beings.

The music they made was no longer the music of exile. To celebrate their first Christmas at home there was an East Anglian performance of Britten's new *Ceremony of Carols*. These settings of early English poems for treble voices and harp are among the loveliest and liveliest of all his works for children and amateurs. There are unforgettable moments of magic: the icy stillness of 'In freezing winter'; the flowing graciousness of the lullaby, 'O my dear heart'; the precipitous entry in canon of 'This little babe' and the overwhelming excitement of the repeated shouts of *Deo gratias*.

In the next year, 1943, he was asked to write a cantata for a parish church. (It was the same church that had commissioned Henry Moore's 'Madonna and Child'.) The request meant a great deal to him for he believed that churches needed artists and artists needed churches. He chose his verses for *Rejoice in the Lamb* from the long poem by Christopher Smart, the deeply religious poet who wrote his best work while he was shut up in a lunatic asylum. The cantata is as unlike conventional church music as it could possibly be. There are unexpected moments when the poet's cat Jeoffry worships God in his way 'by wreathing his body seven times round with elegant quickness'. There is a terrifying moment when the poor mad man hears the cruel shout of 'Silly Fellow! Silly Fellow!' and a moment of unforgettable beauty when he knows that Christ will deliver him out of all his hardships. The exciting rhythm of the dancing procession on page 38

From *Rejoice in the Lamb*, Op. 30

looks difficult on paper, but it is easy and exhilarating to sing when it has been learnt by heart. The rhythm of the spoken words has to give way to the rhythm of the tune, but miraculously the words keep their meaning, and gain rather than lose by being wedded to such individual time-patterns.

During this same summer he was working at his *Serenade* for tenor, horn and strings. He had devised his own text for it, choosing some of his favourite poems about evening, by poets as seemingly far apart as Blake, Ben Jonson and Keats. With great skill he managed to bring the contrasting poems together into a continuous song-cycle, so that the verses, in belonging to his music, belong also to each other. The listeners at the first performance in October 1943 were stirred by this strange new beauty that sounded so right and so inevitable, and several of them felt that the rebirth of English music was happening at last. A few days afterwards, in a letter to a friend, Britten said: 'It is encouraging that you too sense that "something" in the air which heralds a renaissance. I feel terrifically conscious of it. Whether we are the voices crying in the wilderness or the thing itself it isn't for us to know, but anyhow it is so very exciting. It is of course in all the arts, but in music, particularly, it's this acceptance of "freedom" without any arbitrary restrictions, this simplicity, this contact with audiences of our own time and of people like ourselves, this seriousness, and above all this professionalism.'

In using the word 'professionalism' he meant the complete absence of that woolly, muddle-headed vagueness that has always made him so angry. And in speaking of audiences 'like ourselves' he was not just referring to a few trained musicians: he was thinking of the growing number of serious listeners, however inexperienced they might be.

Inexperienced audiences were taking up a great deal of his time just then, for he and Peter Pears were touring England giving wartime recitals in small towns and villages for a ramshackle, poverty-stricken organization which has since been transformed out of all recognition into the Arts Council of Great Britain. Their concerts were often fantastic adventures: they would have to find their way in the pouring rain down some dark, muddy East Anglian lane that was little better than a cart-track, until they eventually reached a desolate, tin-roofed village hall. Here they would find a smoking oil-stove in one corner and in the opposite corner an elderly upright piano with polished brass candle-brackets and panels of fretwork and faded pink silk. In the middle of the hall, huddled close together, would be an audience of twenty or thirty people who had never been to a concert before, but who were enthralled by the singing and playing.

Occasionally the concerts were in prisons. Their friend Michael Tippett has recently written a vivid description of a recital they gave in Wormwood Scrubs while he was imprisoned there as a pacifist. He says: 'I am ashamed to mention the untruthful wangling by which I convinced the authorities that the recital was impossible unless I turned the pages for the pianist. Up to the last moment it was touch and go. But finally I stepped out of the ranks and sat down unexpectedly on the platform beside him. A strange moment for us both. He remembers, I am sure, that huge, primitive and responsive audience of "jail-birds".'

When he had to be in London, Britten shared a flat with his friend Erwin Stein, the music editor at the publishing firm of Boosey and Hawkes. Before the war Stein had lived in Vienna: as a young man he had listened to operas conducted by Mahler and had had composition lessons from Schoenberg and had talked about music with his fellow-students Berg and Webern. He became one of Britten's closest friends. Composers need encouragement, and Erwin Stein was the ideal encourager. Until his death in 1958 he did more than anyone else in helping Britten with all the technical problems that have to be solved if a composer's manuscript is to be accurately engraved for publication.

Throughout 1943 and 1944 Britten went down as often as possible to the mill at Snape which was still his home. His sister Beth was living there with her two small children while her husband was away on war service. It was a peaceful place for a composer to think and write, for there were very few cars in those days. He was able to walk for mile after mile across the commons and marshes, planning his opera *Peter Grimes*. He worked at it all through 1944, and by the beginning of 1945 it was finished.

VIII

Peter Grimes
and the English Opera Group

The opera, *Peter Grimes*, had its first performance at Sadler's Wells on 7th June 1945, a month after the war in Europe had come to an end. It must have needed a good deal of faith to organize the production of a new English opera that year. The Royal Opera House at Covent Garden had been used as a dance hall during the war, and Sadler's Wells had been closed to the public since the bombing of 1940. Some of the members of the Sadler's Wells company had managed to keep together under the directorship of Joan Cross, and they had been touring the provinces with just a few singers and players and technicians. Peter Pears had been working with them since 1943, and when they heard about the opera Britten was writing they decided, with immense courage, that they would produce it in London. They rehearsed it wherever they happened to be: in a Methodist hall in Sheffield, or in a gymnasium in Birmingham. And they learnt the music in the intervals of giving eight performances a week of other operas, while struggling with the discomforts of wartime travel. (In those days a train journey meant standing in the corridor with room for one foot but not for the other.)

The first performance was an overwhelming triumph. No one in the audience will ever forget the excitement of that evening. Here, at last, was a real English opera that was going to live side by side with any of the great operas of the world. The drama in the music was utterly compelling from the first note to the last, and each of the characters had a musical personality. The story moved swiftly: there was no aimless hanging around, yet the singers sang real arias with memorable tunes that could be taken home and whistled. When the action needed the urgency of recitative, the sung conversations had all the directness and energy of their own native language. The huge orchestra never drowned the singers' words, yet when the east-coast storm arose the whole theatre was flooded with wave after wave of

41

The Moot Hall, Aldeburgh, at the time when Crabbe was writing *The Borough*

sound. Actors and audience were aware all the time of the cold, grey sea of Crabbe's poem: when a door at the back of the stage suddenly blew open at the height of the storm, Suffolk listeners sitting in the stalls could feel the north-east draught round their ankles. The music stretched beyond the boxed-in sides of the stage, and when the hostile crowds in the wings called out 'Peter Grimes! . . . Peter *Grimes*!', their voices sounded as if they were coming from far along the coast. In the fog of the terrible man-hunt, the poor demented fisherman seemed to grow in stature until he was no longer a separate individual: like the 'Silly Fellow' of *Rejoice in the Lamb* he was bearing the burden of all those other outcasts who are rejected by their law-abiding neighbours because they are different from other people.

When the tragedy had reached its quiet end and the opera was over, the listeners knew that they had been hearing a masterpiece and that nothing like this had ever happened before in English music. They stood up and shouted and shouted. Hundreds of letters reached the mill at Snape. A fortnight after the first performance Britten wrote to a friend, saying: 'I am so glad that the opera came up to your expectations. I must confess that I am very pleased with the way that it seems to "come over the footlights", and also with the way the audience takes it, and what is perhaps more, returns night after night to take it again! I think the occasion is actually a greater one than either Sadler's Wells or me. Perhaps it is an omen for English Opera in the future. Anyhow, I hope that many composers will take the plunge, and I hope also that they'll find, as I did, the water not quite so icy as expected!'

It was not only in England that *Peter Grimes* made such a deep impression: within the next three years it was translated into Italian, German, Swedish, Danish, Flemish, Czech and Hungarian and was performed in twenty cities, from Milan, Berlin and Budapest to New York, Los Angeles and Sydney.

Two months after that epoch-making first performance, Britten was touring the concentration camps of Germany with Yehudi Menuhin, giving two or three short recitals a day. He found it a terrifying experience to be with so many hundreds of people who had been living so close to death. As soon as he got back to England he 'defied the nightmare horror' by writing his *Holy Sonnets of John Donne* (Op. 35); passionate settings of passionate poems in which death is triumphantly defeated.

He and Peter Pears gave the first performance of the *Holy Sonnets* on St. Cecilia's Day, 1945. Twenty-four hours earlier, Britten had been listening to the first performance of his *String Quartet No. 2* (Op. 36), which he had written to commemorate the two hundred and fiftieth anniversary of the death of Purcell. He has owed more to Purcell than to any other composer, and he still goes on learning from his music, not only from what he has described as the 'clarity, brilliance, tenderness and strangeness' of the songs, but also from the vitality of the instrumental pieces. It was to the tune of one of Purcell's hornpipes that he wrote *The Young Person's Guide to the Orchestra* (Op. 34), that liveliest and most exhilarating of all lessons in instrumentation.

During this time he was already at work on a new opera; a chamber opera with a small orchestra of twelve players. The libretto was founded on the classical story of *The Rape of Lucretia*. Two narrators stood on either side of the stage; they remained outside the action, while bringing to the pagan tragedy the pity and understanding of Christian commentators. At the first performance in July 1946 many of the audience were perplexed and acutely embarrassed. They were aware that beautiful music was going on, but they felt so uncomfortable they could hardly listen to it. 'Why couldn't he be content with what happened in history in 500 B.C.?' they asked. '*Why* drag in Christianity?' But in Britten's mind there was no question of 'dragging in' Christianity: it had been there all the time. He would never have set a cruel subject to music without linking the cruelty to the hope of redemption.

Peter Grimes and the English Opera Group

A few days after this somewhat bewildering first performance he wrote to one of his friends, saying: 'Your understanding of my work, of Lucretia especially, gives me great encouragement. Especially the manner in which you approach the Christian idea delighted me. I used to think that the day when one could shock people was over—but now, I've discovered that being simple and considering things spiritual of importance, produces violent reactions!'

Whatever the critics might have to say about it, the performers knew that what Britten was doing was right. Some of them had been working with him ever since *Peter Grimes*, and they now decided to form their own English Opera Group so that they could continue to produce new chamber operas with a small enough cast and orchestra to take on tour.

It was for the English Opera Group that Britten wrote *Albert Herring* in 1947. This East Suffolk version of a French comedy is peopled with fictitious nineteenth-century characters who are so uproariously entertaining that it is almost impossible not to laugh out loud when one is listening to the music. There is the pompous, tyrannical Lady of the Manor, whose enormous feathered hat is perched high on her head; there is the Police Superintendent who clears his throat on the first beat of the bar; and there is the flutteringly over-anxious schoolmistress, who gives a determined but unhelpful 'One—and—*two*—AND' to her inattentive pupils, whose gaze keeps wandering to the trestle-tables laden with food for the party.

The hero of the opera is a tragic, rather than a comic, figure. Albert serves behind the counter in his mother's greengrocery shop. He is so simple that people laugh at him, or try to bully him. In his own way he is another 'Silly Fellow', and the audience suffers with him in his clumsy and touching doubts and decisions. But all ends happily, and it is the bossy, interfering characters who are discomfited.

The scene of the action in *Albert Herring* is 'a small market-town in East Anglia': references to 'a dance at the Jubilee Hall' and to the outlying villages of Iken and Snape suggest that the market-town might be Aldeburgh. Soon after the first performance of the opera Britten gave up the mill at Snape and went to live in Aldeburgh at No. 4 Crabbe Street, a few yards away from the Jubilee Hall of *Albert Herring* on the one side and the Moot Hall of *Peter Grimes* on the other. His study window had a view straight on to the sea: at high tide it looked as though the waves might come in at any moment. Fishing-boats were drawn up on the long stretch of shingle, and in the early mornings the nets were spread out to dry just beyond his gate. This house was to be his home for the next ten years.

44

IX

The Aldeburgh Festival

On an August day in 1947 Britten was travelling across Europe with members of the English Opera Group who had been performing *Albert Herring* at the Holland Festival and were on their way to perform it at the Lucerne Festival. Half-way between Amsterdam and the Swiss frontier Peter Pears suddenly said: 'Why not make our *own* Festival? A modest Festival, with a few concerts given by friends? Why not have an "Aldeburgh Festival"?' They talked about it for the rest of the journey and as soon as they returned home they began making plans. They called on the Mayor and the Vicar of Aldeburgh, and they invited members of the Town Council to tea and asked them what they thought of the idea.

East Anglians have a reputation for treating newcomers as 'foreigners' and potential enemies: Crabbe mentions in one of his poems that the inhabitants of the Borough used to 'scowl at strangers with suspicious eye'. But on this occasion all went well. Permission was given for concerts to be held in the Parish Church and the Baptist Chapel; several owners of large houses promised to lend their rooms for picture exhibitions, and others offered to give hospitality to singers and players. A public meeting was held in the Jubilee Hall on a cold, wet January evening and £200 was guaranteed. A few weeks later the sum had grown to £1,400, and when the Arts Council gave its official support everyone knew that the Festival was really going to happen. Members of the local amateur dramatic society and the Women's Institute spent day after day addressing envelopes for the advance publicity; in the late spring fresh coats of paint appeared on many of the houses, and by the time it was June and the audiences began to arrive nearly all the houses and shops in the High Street had their window-ledges and balconies decorated with armfuls of flowers, including the beautiful yellow tree-lupins that still grow in profusion at the edge of the marshes.

The Festival began in the church with the first performance of Britten's newly-written cantata *St. Nicolas*. There were more than a hundred singers

45

From *Saint Nicolas*, Op. 42

from East Suffolk in the choir. The music, which had been commissioned for a school, was as dramatic as an opera: each scene in the life of the saint was as clear to follow as if it had been acted on a stage. During Nicolas's journey to Palestine the strings, pianos and percussion conjured up a tremendous storm at sea: the tenors' and basses' desperate shouts of 'Shorten sail! Reef her! *Heave* her to!' were almost lost at the crest of each wave as the cymbal's reverberations floundered and splashed and spilled over. In the scene representing Nicolas's birth and childhood there was a light-hearted waltz which made the listeners sit up in amazement: they said afterwards that they hadn't ever expected to hear such 'pious frivolity' in a church. During the last verse of this waltz-tune there was a wonderful moment when the boy Nicolas left his childhood behind him and the piping treble voice of the smallest choir-boy, singing 'God be glorified!' was transformed into the full, ringing voice of the tenor soloist, with all its strength and confidence. But the crowning glory of the work came at the end, when the listeners were drawn into the singing of 'God moves in a mysterious way', and the 'frozen hearts' in the audience-congregation became unfrozen.

St. Nicholas was a perfect beginning for the ten days of music. And by the tenth day it was obvious that the Aldeburgh Festival was going to happen every year.

At the second Festival, in 1949, the new work was Britten's short opera for children, *The Little Sweep*, or *Let's make an Opera*. The Suffolk story was set in the neighbouring village of Iken, and the leading characters, aged eight to fourteen, were called after the sons and daughters and nephews of the Festival chairman. Members of the audience found that they were expected to sing four of the songs themselves; in fact, they were responsible for providing the overture, two entractes, and the final chorus. (We take these 'Audience Songs' for granted today, but they caused a hubbub of excited comment at the first performance in 1949, when hardened opera-goers anxiously clutched their song-sheets, exclaiming: 'What! In *five-four?*' or '*What?* Diminished octaves?') Luckily they were given a chance of rehearsing their songs during the first part of the entertainment. This helped, particularly in the 'Night Song', where the voices were divided into four choirs, each representing a different bird: the owls were asked to sing 'Tu-whoo!' while the herons cried 'Kaah!', the doves murmured 'Prrr-ooo!' and the chaffinches squeaked 'Pink! Pink! Pink!' (The dividing-up caused further consternation: a tall, thin music critic rose to the occasion by waving his tightly-rolled umbrella and calling out to the conductor: 'Excuse me, but where did you say the *herons* should be?') Everyone managed to

Andante tenebroso

Audience

The owl, wide wing-ing through the sky, In search of mice and les-ser fry, Re-peats his long un-hap-py cry — To-whoo!.. To-whoo!.. To-whoo!.. To-whoo!.. (etc.)

learn the tunes remarkably quickly, and the final 'Coaching Song' was a triumph; the children on the stage improvised a coach with the nursery rocking-horse and a couple of chairs; the eight-year-olds twirled parasols round and round to the rhythm of the wheels, while the whole Jubilee Hall was filled with the trotting and the cantering of the percussion.

Ever since those early years the Festival has succeeded in being festive, and has always provided something belonging by rights to Aldeburgh more than to anywhere else. There have been 'domestic' events which could only have happened in the Jubilee Hall or the Parish Church: Britten playing the one note on his viola in Purcell's 'Fantazia upon one Note', or Menuhin sitting among the first violins in the orchestra and sharing a music-stand in a Brandenburg concerto.

Peter Pears's idea of 'a few concerts given by friends' still holds good. The list of friends is impressively long: there have been first performances of works specially written for the occasion by Michael Tippett, William Walton, Lennox Berkeley, Roberto Gerhard, Priaulx Rainier and Hans Werner Henze; exhibitions of pictures and sculpture by Henry Moore, John Piper and Georg Ehrlich; and lectures by E. M. Forster, William Plomer, Edith Sitwell, Kenneth Clark, Francis Poulenc and Aaron Copland. Local events have included talks on 'The Sutton Hoo Ship Burial'; 'Sailing in East Anglia'; 'Change Ringing' (illustrated by the local bell-ringers) and an open-air exhibition of deep-sea fishing-tackle arranged on the beach by Britten's fisherman friend, Bill Burrell.

One year there was a celebration of the bi-centenary of the birth of Crabbe; after a lunch with speeches at the East Suffolk Hotel, coachloads of visitors were taken to the various houses in the neighbourhood where the poet had stayed with friends or acquaintances, ending up with a tea-party at Great Glemham House (the home of the original Gay, Juliet, Sophie, Tina and Hughie of *The Little Sweep*) where Crabbe had lived at the end of the eighteenth century.

On another occasion there was an evening of 'Wine and Song' in the crowded Workmen's Club at Thorpeness, where Herr Andreas von Schubert's superb wine from the Maximin Grünhaus vineyard was tasted to the superb sound of Franz Schubert's music. As Peter Pears said, 'we could echo the words written about those far-off days with Schubert in Vienna, for "we were the happiest people in all the world: and it was not only to the Schubert songs we owed it, but also to the splendid, modest, warm-hearted people who were together then!" '

It is certainly owing to the splendid, warm-hearted people in Aldeburgh that Benjamin Britten and Peter Pears have been able to make the Festival happen every year since 1948. How could they have known, in those early days, that they would find such skilled stage-carpenters working in Crabbe Street or such willing washers-up living on Crag Path? How could they guess that Mr. Paul Beck, lodging in a three-roomed cottage in Neptune Alley, was one of the best piano-tuners in the whole of England? When he died in 1959, Britten wrote in the Festival programme book: 'To see him at work was a lesson to us all. Calm at the most tense moments between the last anxious rehearsal and the admittance of the audience; patiently waiting at the crack of dawn for the church doors to be opened to prepare a harpsichord; soothing and helping a nervous performer before and during a performance (I speak from personal experience)—all this was the sign of the true artist. Since the first days of the first Festival he had become the warm and trusted friend of us all. He will be most sadly missed.' He has, indeed, been missed. But his successor from London immediately proved to be as true an artist and as trusted a friend; helping to move the heaviest platforms into position; finding lost music stands; steering unauthorized photographers out of the way; dealing with all those furious visitors who keep on asking, '*Why* are there no tickets left?'; and taking urgent messages to soloists whose landladies have not got a telephone.

The 'modest' Festival of 1948 has grown in many ways but it has never become grand. First-night audiences, during the intervals of an opera, can still step out on to the pebbly beach, breathing lungfuls of north-east wind as they stand in the shelter of the life-boat. The Jubilee Hall still holds only just over three hundred people, although it has been enlarged since the

1948 performance of *Albert Herring* when there was no room in the orchestra pit for the harp or the percussion and they had to be played in the auditorium, with a screen round the harp and a barrier of brightly-coloured eiderdowns draped round the drums. The Parish Church is no longer large enough to hold the audiences for orchestral concerts, so they are given in the neighbouring medieval churches of Orford and Blythburgh. Here the doors can be kept wide open during performances, for there is no main-road traffic to disturb the players, and nobody minds if the singing of the birds occasionally gets mixed up with the notes of a Haydn symphony.

Keeping the Festival 'modest' means working hard to cut down the expenses, and a good deal of Britten's time is taken up with practical questions such as 'Can we do without a third trumpet and a second bassoon?' Planning goes on for eleven months of the year, and nearly every week there are business meetings at Britten's home. This is no longer the house on the edge of the sea: it is now an old farm-house nearly a mile from Aldeburgh, with a large walled garden, and warm rooms filled with exciting pictures and sculpture. Our Festival discussions often go on until midnight, for we have to struggle with the usual problems that beset all organizers: dates being altered without warning in a foreign opera house; the sudden illness of a singer, or the obstinate refusal of a player to answer letters and telegrams. Peter Pears joins us at week-ends and bank holidays, whenever he is free from his London concerts or his foreign tours, and however difficult our problems may have seemed, he is always able to solve them for us. Britten's housekeeper, Miss Hudson, has never failed to provide wonderful meals for any number of people at any hour of the night, so that committee meetings have a way of turning into parties, with home-bottled wine fetched from the cellar and poured out by candle-light.

Visitors to Aldeburgh sometimes ask how Britten is able to give so much time to planning the Festival when his life as a composer is already so full. But composers cannot remain shut up in a room thinking about their own works all the time. They need live people to talk to and live performances of the music they love. It is worth all the time and thought and energy that Britten spends on the Festival when June arrives and he is able to do the right music with the right people in the right place.

PLATE III

(a) *Britten at work in his studio*

(b) *Rehearsing the chorus for* A Midsummer Night's Dream *in the Jubilee Hall, Aldeburgh, 1960*

PLATE IV

The beginning of a walk, from just outside his garden gate

X

Composing and Performing

Composers are not a different sort of people from 'ordinary' people. The things they express in their music are the things that 'ordinary' people think and feel, but a composer's thinking and feeling has to go much deeper. Britten mentioned this in a speech he made in 1951, when he was given the Freedom of Lowestoft. 'Artists are artists', he said, 'because they have an extra sensitivity—a skin less, perhaps, than other people; and the great ones have an uncomfortable habit of being right about many things, long before their time. . . . So when you hear of an artist saying or doing something strange or unpopular, think of that extra sensitivity—that skin less; consider a moment whether he may not after all be seeing a little more clearly than ourselves, whether he is really as irresponsible as he seems, before you condemn him. Remember for a moment Mozart in his pauper's grave; Dostoievsky sent to Siberia; Blake ridiculed as a madman, Lorca shot by the Fascists in Spain. It is a proud privilege to be a creative artist, but it can also be painful.'

In the same speech he said: 'As an artist, I want to serve the community. . . . In other days, artists were the servants of institutions like the Church, or of private patrons. Today it is the community (or all of us in our own small ways) that orders the artist about. And I do not think that is such a bad thing, either. It is not a bad thing for an artist to try to serve all sorts of different people . . . [and] to have to work to order. Any artist worth his salt has ideas knocking about in his head, and an invitation to write something can often direct these ideas into a concrete form and shape. Of course, it can sometimes be difficult when one doesn't feel in the mood, but perhaps that's good for one, too!—anyhow, composers (like other people) can be horribly lazy, and often this is the only way that they can be made to produce something.'

Writing to order was the way all composers worked until the nineteenth century: it was only then that people began thinking that art should be 'useless' and that composers ought to wait until they felt 'inspired'. Whenever anyone asks Britten about inspiration he always assures them that 'nothing comes of itself'. 'Everything', he says, 'is the result of hard work and technique.'

Technique, in composing, means finding the right notes. This may not seem very difficult, but there is more to it than just finding the right notes when making up a short tune: that is what Britten could do when he was seven, and it is what any musical seven-year-old can do. The 'concrete shape' of a symphony or a string quartet has to be planned as carefully as the concrete shape of a cathedral. And in the working out of the plan on paper, every detail has to be exactly right or the whole structure may be in danger of collapse.

The search for the right notes keeps Britten working very hard for hour after hour and day after day. He usually writes every morning from about 8.30 to 12.30; then he takes the manuscript to the piano and plays through what he has written. He goes back to work at about 4, and keeps at it till 7.30 or 8 in the evening. During his hours off in the afternoon he plays tennis, or swims. Or he takes his two small dachshunds for a walk on the marshes, or along the beach at Shingle Street, or beyond the ruined walls of Dunwich where a whole medieval city has sunk out of sight under the sea. Here he listens in his mind's ear to the way the notes he has written that morning are taking their place in the over-all shape of the music. This shape may have been in his thoughts for many months before he began putting anything down on paper.

If he is writing an opera he begins by having long talks with his librettist. They discuss the story in detail and plan the whole work, as Britten himself has described it, 'in the way that an artist might block out a picture', dividing it into scenes and even into arias, recitatives and choruses. When the librettist has finished his first draft of the words, Britten goes through it with him very carefully, pointing out any weak syllables that might interfere with the rhythm of a tune, or any clusters of consonants that might prevent the singing from being smooth enough at an expressive moment in the drama.

It was while he was still having discussions with William Plomer about the libretto for his opera *Gloriana* that I first began working for him in Aldeburgh. My job was to copy out his pencil sketches of the music for each scene as soon as he had finished writing it, and to make a piano arrangement that the singers could use at rehearsals. I already knew that he was as practical a composer as my father had been, but even so it was

March from *Gloriana*, Op. 53

Lively marching tempo ($\text{♩}=88$)

astonishing to see how strictly he could keep to his time-schedule of work. He was able to say in the middle of October, when he was just beginning Act I, that he would have finished the second act before the end of January. It was like hearing a builder say when a new house would be ready to live in, except that builders nearly always finish later than they have promised; but there could be no delay over the opera, as it had been commissioned to celebrate the coronation of Queen Elizabeth II, and the date of the first performance at Covent Garden had already been fixed for 8th June 1953. He managed to keep to his time-schedule in spite of the disastrous interruption of the East Coast floods in January, when the sea reached the windows on one side of his Crabbe Street house and the river came in at the doors on the other side.

When he began work on the full score of the opera, he wrote at such a tremendous speed that I thought I should never keep pace with him. He managed to get through at least twenty vast pages a day, and it seemed as if he never had to stop and think. (The only occasions when I had a chance of catching up with him were when he happened to notice a rare bird flying out to sea: he would then break off work for a few minutes to look at it through his binoculars.)

While he was still working on the full score of *Gloriana* he was already thinking about his next opera, *The Turn of the Screw*, which had been commissioned for the Venice Festival of 1954. This was to be a chamber opera, with instrumental variations linking each of the sixteen short scenes. John Piper was designing the stage set. He knew that the music was to be continuous, so he arranged to have gauze curtains that could be drawn across any part of the stage between one scene and the next, so that the same set could be used for several different scenes: at the entrance to a house; through a window; on a tower; by a lake; or outside a church.

The music of *The Turn of the Screw* was written with very little time to spare. The vocal score had to be copied out straight away in batches of half a dozen pages and posted to London the same day: it seemed incredible that a composer could be so sure of what he wanted that he would risk parting with the beginning of a scene before he had written the end of it. The battle against time was won, though the orchestral parts were finished only twenty minutes before the first rehearsal.

Keeping to the time-schedule for each new work would be fairly easy if it were not for the fact that Britten is a performer as well as a composer. His recitals with Peter Pears take up several months in the year: sometimes they are abroad for six strenuous weeks on end, giving as many as four

High Street, Aldeburgh, from the Terrace

concerts in five days before moving on to the next city.

Of all that has been said about Britten's piano playing, nothing is more appropriate than the remark made by the great Russian cellist Rostropovitch when he said 'Britten-the-pianist closely resembles Britten-the-composer'. He plays songs by Schubert or Haydn or Verdi with such intimate concern that the music sounds as if it were his own. It is the same with his conducting. The word 'interpretation' never comes into anyone's mind when he conducts Mozart or Mahler or Tchaikovsky or any of the other great composers whose works are necessary to his well-being.

He learnt to conduct by having to take charge, often against his will, of first performances of his own works. In twenty years' experience—some of it painful—he has discovered how to make his beat so clear that it can convey the music itself and can draw superlative playing from the orchestra he is working with. Any rehearsal he takes is a lesson in how to avoid wasting time. Every detail has been thought out beforehand: the family motto of 'Never unprepared' is still very much to the point. This does not mean that he is inflexible in his ideas. On one occasion, while he was conducting the final rehearsal of a Mozart symphony, he suddenly realized that the usual bowing in the Minuet was the wrong way round, so he stopped in the middle of the movement and asked the strings to change all the up-bows to down and all the down-bows to up. The players looked a bit surprised, and he had to apologize for not having thought of it earlier. But as soon as they tried it over they realized that it was obviously right.

It is no wonder that every year there are more and more requests for him to conduct other orchestras. He has to refuse most of them, because

55

PAN, from *Six Metamorphoses after Ovid*, Op. 49

Senza misura

there is so little time for composing. He already finds it difficult enough to fit in everything that has to be done. He never wastes a minute on his frequent journeys. He dislikes air-travel, but he can't always avoid it, so he spends the time correcting proofs and revising scores for republication. He can plan a new work while sitting in the back of a car, and he often thinks and occasionally writes in a train. (The thirteen-part fugue in *The Turn of the Screw* was written between Ipswich and Liverpool Street, and for once his very clear manuscript was quite difficult to decipher.)

Travelling is the least tiring part of being on tour. The hospitality is much more exhausting. Parties are given after concerts, and hosts have been known to keep their artists standing for two hours on end; introducing them to one person after another; offering them drinks, but never thinking of offering them any solid food.

Then there are the press photographers. These can be particularly distracting during a recording session. A conductor has no chance to relax when he is recording, for during the fifteen-minute break for coffee he has to listen to a play-back of the tapes in the balance room, before returning to the studio and encouraging his players and asking them to try the same bit just once more.

All this is part of the normal life of a performer. But Britten has to lead the double life of a composer-performer. And when he is half-way through a new work and has to leave Aldeburgh for a concert tour the interruption can be almost unbearable. There is nothing that can be done about it, and there is no way in which his friends can console him. Miss Hudson has always done all that she can to help; coming to the door to wave good-bye in the early morning, and saying 'Have you got your passport? Have you got your money? Have you remembered all the music you'll need?' (The two dachshunds never appear on these occasions: they go and bury their heads in their baskets, because partings are too painful and there is no way of knowing whether the journey is only to Amsterdam or right across to Vancouver.) After a few days or weeks a postcard finds its way to Aldeburgh, from perhaps six thousand miles away, saying: '*Phew!* this is hard work, but everyone is endlessly kind.'

Holidays are rare, but occasionally there are visits to Switzerland for ski-ing, and once there was a journey from Aldeburgh to the Rhine in a motor launch skippered by Bill Burrell and his brother. Recital tours can sometimes be combined with a holiday, as in the winter of 1955–6, when they had a memorable journey to the Far East. 'We spent Christmas gazing at the Taj Mahal!' he wrote. 'We were touched and moved greatly by the

Indians' grace, beauty, warmth and oh . . . their *calm!* The way they squat on their heels and do nothing for hours; how I wish I could do that.' A fortnight later there was a letter from Bali saying: 'After a week of hectic concerts in Java we came on here—the island where musical sounds are as [much] part of the atmosphere as the palm trees, the spicy smells, and the charming beautiful people. The music is *fantastically* rich—melodically, rhythmically, texture (such *orchestration!*) and above all *formally.* . . . At last I'm beginning to catch on to the technique, but it's about as complicated as Schoenberg.' (The Balinese technique has since then worked its way into his own music. He has borrowed the gradual *ad lib.* accelerando, from very slow to very quick, on tremolando repeated notes. And he has been influenced by the texture of the *gamelan* orchestra, where each instrument plays a variant of the same short, five-note tune, coming in at a different place and at a different speed, so that the tune provides its own harmony and counterpoint, extending far beyond its original length. The exciting Balinese rhythms sound like free improvisations, but they are strictly organized and disciplined: each individual player is responsible for keeping the whole structure together, for the orchestra has no conductor.)

Bali was 'a glorious 12 days' holiday'. They went on to Tokyo to give more concerts, and there they heard and saw a performance of a traditional Japanese Nō play. One of the friends who was with them described it in his travel diary that same night: 'The play is about the Sumida river: the ferryman is waiting in his boat, a traveller turns up and tells him about a woman who will soon be coming to the river. The woman is mad, she is looking for her lost child. Then she appears and the ferryman does not wish to take a mad person, but in the end he lets her into his boat. On the way across the river the two passengers sit behind each other on the floor as if in a narrow boat, while the ferryman stands behind them, symbolically punting with a light stick. The ferryman tells the story of a little boy who came this way a year ago this very day. The child was very tired for he had escaped from robbers who had held him. He crossed the river in this boat, but he died from exhaustion on the other side. The woman starts crying. It was her son. The ferryman is sorry for her and takes her to the child's grave. The mother is acted by a tall man in woman's clothing with a small woman's mask on his face. Accessories help you to understand what is going on: a bamboo branch in the hand indicates madness, a long stick is the ferryman's punting pole, a very small gong is beaten for the sorrowing at the graveside. As soon as these props are no longer necessary, stage-hands who have brought them to the actors take them away again.'

Composing and Performing

This play made a tremendous impression on Britten. The economy of the style, the slowness of the action and the strange mixture of chanting and singing were an entirely new 'operatic' experience. He came back to England knowing that he would one day write the music for an East Anglian version of the same story.

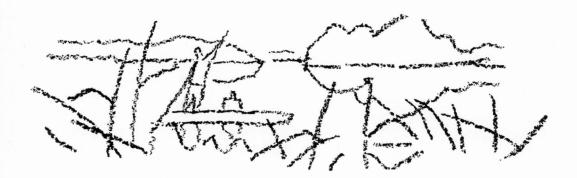

XI

Amateurs and Professionals

A few months after he had returned home from the Far East he happened to listen to a concert in Aldeburgh Church given by several hundred East Suffolk school-children. The eight-year-olds from the borders of Norfolk sang folk songs and his own 'New Year Carol' from *Friday Afternoons*, and hearing the sound of all those very young voices in that building, he decided that he would write something for children to sing and play and act in a church. The result was *Noye's Fludde*. The medieval Chester Miracle Play made a perfect libretto. There was no need to modernize the spelling, for it added its own contribution to the liveliness of the long lists of beasts and birds that joined the procession into the ark. (He was delighted to discover our local 'curlues' and 'redshanckes' among them.) He kept all the comic scenes, including Mrs. Noye boxing her husband's ears and Noye's rebounding protest of 'Ha! marye, this is hotte!' The headmistress who had doubts about allowing her girls to be Gossips because they had to reel to and fro shouting, 'Drink! *Drink!* DRINK!' need not, after all, have worried so much, for the whole performance was as deeply moving as the 'pious frivolity' of *St. Nicolas*.

As in *St. Nicolas*, the members of the audience-congregation were given several hymns to sing in *Noye's Fludde*, not just as extras, but as an essential part of the drama: in fact, it was their singing of 'Eternal Father' at the climax of the storm that made the wind drop and the waters subside. The nine professional instrumentalists were surrounded by an enormous orchestra of boys and girls. There were special parts for third violins and second cellos who had not been learning very long. Pizzicato open strings, played with deliberate precision, were just right for Noye's first hammer-strokes in building the ark. When the storm rose and the rigging began to flap in the wind, the vigorous 'slap-slap-slap-slap' of the repeated down-bows and percussion sounded exactly like the wet cord that beats against the flagstaff by the Aldeburgh Moot Hall during a January gale. The high, piercing

An Aldeburgh family rehearsing for a meeting of the Music Club at Britten's house

trills of the recorders, moving chromatically upwards, brought the gale uncomfortably close. Britten kept a descant and a treble recorder on his table all the time he was writing the storm-music, so that he could try out the fingering for each trill. Being an amateur recorder player himself, he knew all about the difficulties of the instrument. (At meetings of the Aldeburgh Music Club there are still occasions, during the tuning-up, when he can be heard asking in a panic-stricken whisper: 'How do I get A flat?')

He had thought of having teacups hit with a teaspoon for the sound of the first raindrops falling on the roof of the ark. But he came round to me one afternoon saying that he'd tried it out at teatime and it wouldn't work. So I took him into my kitchen and showed him how a row of mugs could be slung on a length of string and hit with a large wooden spoon. We then went along High Street to Mrs. Beech's shop and bought a lot of mugs with 'A Present from Aldeburgh' on them, and he took them the next day to the school at Woolverstone Hall where the boys were already rehearsing the percussion parts.

The handbell players came from nearer home. Britten had happened to invite several members of the Aldeburgh Youth Club to choose what they wanted from among the stamps on the foreign letters that reach him by nearly every post. When the boys mentioned that they had a handbell practice that evening he asked them to come and play to him. And he was so enchanted by the sound that he gave them a part to play at the supreme moment of the drama in *Noye's Fludde*, when the rainbow appears in the sky and the Voice of God promises that all wrath and vengeance shall cease in the newly-washed world.

No other sound could have suited that moment so well; which helps to prove that composers need amateurs just as much as amateurs need composers. Britten did not write all those parts for open strings and mugs and handbells for the sole reason of keeping his players happy: he wrote them because those were the sounds he wanted. The simple, 'obvious' music had to be written with the utmost skill, for it was not easy to persuade the nineteenth-century harmonies of 'Eternal Father' to emerge from such a twentieth-century storm, or to make the bugles' key of B flat and the handbells' key of E flat fit so convincingly into the G major of the final procession to Tallis's eight-part canon. The cleverness, as always, is disguised. There is no need for the audience to recognize that the tune for the Dove's return to the ark has the same notes as for the outward journey but played backwards: the sense of homecoming is in the sound of the music, and it does not depend on the listeners' academic booklearning.

It was *Noye's Fludde* that the Cambridge University Orator had in his mind in 1959 when he introduced Britten as an honorary Doctor of Music, saying: 'He likes composing works on commission—a rare quality—and still more, composing for his *alter ego*, the distinguished singer Peter Pears. Although his works are of a most subtle originality, and are indeed approved by the *avant-garde*, yet they are not lost on the less instructed. And there is no one for whom he makes music more readily than for boys and girls.'

SWISS CLOCK from *Alpine Suite*, 1955

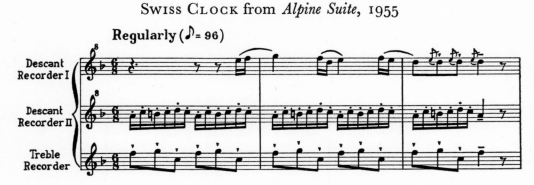

Amateurs and Professionals

In the following year the members of the Cambridge University Music Society gave their new Mus. D. a tumultuous welcome at the first English performance of his *Cantata Academica*, a work commissioned for the six-hundredth anniversary of the foundation of Basle University. The music is filled with sheer enjoyment and is infinitely removed from the old dry-as-dust notions about speech days. With light-hearted skill he gives his singers and players the sort of counterpoint that is a holiday in itself, from the *vivace* fugue with its entries on each of the twelve notes within the octave, to the expressive murmur of the student tenors' and basses' traditional Swiss song that spreads nostalgically beneath the clear cantabile of the professional soprano soloist.

This mixture of amateur and professional brings out the characteristic best in each. He always gives his singers what they will most enjoy doing, as in the Scherzo of the *Spring Symphony*, where the long, lyrical phrases of the solo soprano float high above the raucously energetic 'chop-cherry, chop-cherry' of the boys' voices in unison. Here, and in the choruses of *Noye's Fludde*, the boys need have no more training than they can pick up from regular singing-classes under an intelligent teacher who will encourage them to pronounce their words clearly and who will allow them to sing right out from their chests. But Britten also writes for boys whose voices have been thoroughly trained, as in the *Missa Brevis* he wrote for the Westminster Cathedral Choristers and their choirmaster George Malcolm.

Britten shares his friend George Malcolm's loathing of 'the familiar cooing-sound' of those choir-boys who pronounce 'Amen' as if it were written 'aw-mern'; and he has an equally passionate dislike of the sort of choirmaster who believes that 'a boy's voice must somehow be *rendered harmless* before it can be let loose'.

In his operas he has written some of his most exacting music for boys' voices: the twelve-year-old members of the chorus in *A Midsummer Night's Dream* have to have the technique of soloists. These boys are not amateurs: they are criticized during rehearsals as relentlessly as if they were grown-up professionals.

'Relentless' may seem a strange word to use of anyone as sensitive and patient as Britten. But it is the right word. The professional singers and players who work with him are not just 'good' musicians: they have to be superlatively good, and they have to be prepared to go on getting better and better all the time. There can never be any possibility of a compromise, because the music always comes first.

It is this, more than anything else, that has helped to make him a great composer: it has helped more than his ear, or his invention, or his capacity for hard work. For it has saved him from dividing his energies among all the other things that matter so much to him. To any convinced pacifist it must have been intolerable to have to sit still during all these years and to look on while other pacifists were imprisoned and to see armaments being piled up in one country after another. But Britten has managed to cling to his belief that it is his job to go on making music, and this certainty has enabled him to write his *War Requiem*.

The tremendous 'warning' of the *War Requiem* has been heard and recognized by millions of people all over the world. The whole of his experience went to the making of it, from the promise of peace in *Noye's Fludde* to the cruel, senseless pursuit of the 'Silly Fellow' in *Peter Grimes* and the first remembered sound of the bomb that fell just across the road at Lowestoft during the First World War.

'Ordinary' listeners have understood the meaning of the music, and have been overwhelmed by the sincerity of the work. But sincerity is not enough: the warning of the *War Requiem* needed to be conveyed by a composer who also possesses, in abundance, the self-criticism and authority of the true professional.

Agnus Dei from *Missa Brevis*, Op. 63

Slow and solemn (♩ = 60)

XII

Today and Tomorrow

Abiography of someone who is very much alive can never have a satisfactory last chapter. The catalogue of Britten's works that was brought out on his fiftieth birthday was already out of date a couple of weeks after it had been published.

Several writers on music considered this fiftieth anniversary a suitable opportunity for 'assessing' his works. This may have had its uses, but it created a false impression of a sort of hiatus in the composer's working life, suggesting that he was having to stand aside and mark time while the assessing went on.

No one in Aldeburgh was aware of any such breathing-space during the autumn and winter of 1963. One working day followed another. The *War Requiem*, Op. 66, had immediately been followed by *Psalm 150*, Op. 67, written for the centenary of the foundation of his old prep school. (At the first performance the trumpet part in the *ad lib.* school orchestra was played, with great success, on the mouth-organ.) *Psalm 150* had been followed by the *Cantata Misericordium*, commissioned for the centenary of the International Red Cross, and first performed in Geneva in September 1963: it was one of the most beautiful works he had yet written. And he was preparing for the first performance in Moscow of the *Cello Symphony* he had written for Rostropovitch, as well as thinking about his new work for the next Aldeburgh Festival, during those three months when so many birthday concerts were being given in his honour.

The warmth of welcome that greeted him at all these concerts was something that can seldom have been experienced in twentieth-century England. In the crowded audiences there were one or two people who murmured their doubts about whether so much success was good for a living composer. But they need not have been anxious, for Britten himself had provided the answer in an article that appeared in a Sunday newspaper a few days before his birthday. 'People', he wrote, 'sometimes seem to think that with a number of works now lying behind, one must be bursting with confidence. It is not so at all. I haven't yet achieved the simplicity I should like to in my music, and am enormously aware that I haven't yet come up to the technical standards Bridge set me.'

Among the many honours he has received during the last few years, the one that probably gave him most pleasure was being granted the Freedom of Aldeburgh. The ceremony took place in the Moot Hall. The Mayor in his gold chain of office and the Town Clerk with his silver mace were at the high table; the members of the Town Council sat in the centre of the room, while friends and neighbours crowded round them, filling every available inch of space in the building. After the Vicar had prayed for continual blessings on the new Freeman, the Mayor said: 'No one could describe us as being effusive, and fame in other places means little to the people of Aldeburgh. Those who come to set us right and show us their ways achieve but little. But those who come without fanfares, without wanting to change us all, in short, those who come, however famous, and accept us as we are, very soon become part of our life. And this is true of Mr. Britten. We know him as a quiet, unassuming member of the community, who has given much and asked but little.'

In his reply, Britten said: 'I am proud because this honour comes from people who know me, many of whom have known me for quite a long time too, because although I didn't have the luck to be born here in Aldeburgh, I have in fact lived all my life within thirty miles of it. As I understand it, this honour is not given because of a reputation, because of a chance acquaintance; it is—dare I say it—because you really know me, and accept me as one of yourselves, as a useful part of the borough; and this is, I think, the highest possible compliment for an artist. I believe that an artist should be part of his community, should work for it, with it, and be used by it. Over the last hundred years this has become rarer and rarer and the artist and the community have both suffered as a result. The artist has suffered in many cases because without an audience, or with only a highbrow one —without, therefore, a direct contact with his public—his work tends to become "ivory tower", without focus. This has made a great deal of modern work obscure and impractical: only useable by highly skilled performers and only understandable by the most erudite. Don't please think that I am against all new and strange ideas. Far from it; new ideas have a way of seeming odd and surprising when heard for the first time. But I am against experiment for experiment's sake, originality at all costs. It's necessary to say this because there are audiences who are not discriminating about it.

From *Nocturnal after John Dowland*, Op. 70

They think that everything new is good; that if it is shocking it must be important. There is all the difference in the world between Picasso, the great, humble artist, or Henry Moore, and the chap who slings paint on canvas; between Stravinsky and electronic experimenters. . . .'

Electronic devices leave him utterly cold: his music will always need human beings to sing or play it. No one can tell what he will write in future, but it is safe to predict that he will go on giving his singers and players what they can enjoy (and that in doing so, he will stretch their existing technique beyond their furthest imagining); that he will always construct his works on a basis of sounds and never on theories; that he will extend the possibilities of keys and chords without ever abandoning them (so that there will never be a time when the harmonies of 'Eternal Father' are no longer a part of his musical language); that each new work will be unexpected; that he will never forget to write something for beginners; that there will always be magic in the sound of his music; that he will go on writing dramatic works, for he is first and foremost a composer for the stage (though the stage may be in a church as often as it is in a theatre); and that however tragic his texts may be, his music will always convey, in Rostropovitch's words, 'the joy of life and the hope for happiness'.

It is useless to wonder what listeners will be saying about his music in a hundred years' time. We can only know what he and his works mean, here and now, to those musicians who are best able to judge. Michael Tippett has said: 'What does Britten mean to *me*? First; of all the musicians I have met, he is the most sheerly musical. Music seems to flow out of his mind, out of his body. . . . Secondly, he is so vibrantly alive. Within the greyness of so much modern music, his sounds shine. This aliveness belongs always to the future. I am endlessly curious for what may come next. Thirdly . . . he has an innate tenderness and generosity (though he rightly refuses to be bullied).'

It is this generosity that is possibly the chief danger to his work as a composer. There are so many young musicians (the youngest to date is seven and a half) who write to him, not just once, but many times, sending their compositions for him to read, or asking his advice about whom they should learn with or what job they should try for. But perhaps, after all, it is a mistake to worry about it. Anyone who can organize his own music as well as he can should be trusted to organize his own life equally well.

At this moment, in the late spring of 1964, he is working long hours every day, rehearsing his *Curlew River*, 'a Parable for church performance' that is based on the Japanese Nō play he saw and heard in Tokyo.

A fragment from *Curlew River*, Op. 71

The rehearsals are full of problems, for the rhythm of the music is as freely flowing as if it were improvised, and each individual singer and player is responsible for keeping everything together, as there is no conductor. But in spite of the difficulties, he is able to find time to walk across the marshes to the river, and to listen to the real curlews, and to think about the music that is waiting to be written next.

Postscript

While this book was being prepared for press, some of the music that was 'waiting to be written' at the end of Chapter 12 was both written and performed. After *Curlew River*, Op. 71, the next work was the *Suite for Cello*, Op. 72, written by Britten in November and December 1964 for his friend Rostropovitch. A few months later he wrote his Op. 73, the *Gemini Variations* on a theme of Kodály, for flute, violin and piano duet. In a programme note he himself has described how the work came to be composed: 'When we were in Budapest in 1964 we were very taken by a meeting of one of the Music Clubs for schoolchildren—particularly by the versatile gifts of two young twins. They each played the piano, one the violin, the other the flute, they sang, they sight-read, they answered difficult musical questions. At the end of the meeting they approached me and charmingly, if forcefully, asked me to write them a work. My plea of being very busy was gently brushed aside, but I insisted on one small bargaining point. I would do it if they would write me a long letter telling me all about themselves, their work and their play in English. I felt safe. After a week or so, however, the letter arrived in vivid and idiosyncratic language. I felt I must honour my promise'. The twelve-year-old twins came to the 1965 Aldeburgh Festival to give the first performance, playing by heart and changing instruments in mid-movement before an audience that included Kodály as our guest of honour. (Fortunately for other, less versatile, instrumentalists, this 'Quartet for two players' can be performed by *four* musicians.)

Opus 74 was the *Songs and Proverbs of William Blake*, written in March and April 1965 for the great singer Dietrich Fischer-Dieskau.

In August 1965, while Britten was on holiday in Armenia, he set some Pushkin to music in order to improve his Russian. Before leaving England he had happened to buy a paperback edition of Pushkin's poems on the way to the airport: it had the verse in Russian with an English prose translation at the foot of each page. He chose six poems which he asked his Russian friends to read aloud to him, and the result was *Echo Poeta* ('The Poet's Echo'), 'a dialogue between the poet and the unresponsiveness of the natural world he describes': it was performed in Moscow early in October 1965.

A few weeks later, on October 24th, there were simultaneous first performances in London, Paris and New York of *Voices for Today*, Op. 75, a choral work written for the twentieth anniversary of the United Nations. The performances were broadcast during a weekend of political tension in Asia and Africa, and thousands of listeners heard the singing of a sequence of tremendous sentences appealing for international peace, which range from the urgency of 'If you have ears to hear, then hear' to the stern warning of 'Telling lies to the young is wrong', and end with the final message of hope: 'The world's great age begins anew, The golden years return'.

November, 1965.

Index

The titles of Britten's works mentioned in the text are listed together under his name. Music examples are indicated by page numbers in italic type.

Index

Index